Overcoming Emotional
Obstacles through Faith

Overcoming Emotional Obstacles through Faith

Navigating the *Mind* Field

ANTHONY P. ACAMPORA

RESOURCE *Publications* · Eugene, Oregon

OVERCOMING EMOTIONAL OBSTACLES THROUGH
FAITH
Navigating the Mind Field

Resource Publications
An Imprint of Wipf and Stock Publishers
199 W. 8th Ave., Suite 3
Eugene, OR 97401

www.wipfandstock.com

PAPERBACK ISBN: 978-1-5326-1972-4
HARDCOVER ISBN: 978-1-4982-4625-5
EBOOK ISBN: 978-1-4982-4624-8

Manufactured in the U.S.A.   JULY 24, 2017

Dedication

This book is dedicated to my father Peter L. Acampora, affectionately known as "Leeboy." He was given the name when he was a little boy when his cousin—who had a heavy Italian accent—would attempt to call him "Petie-Boy," and it sounded more like "Leeboy." I began lovingly calling him Leeboy right after he shared that heartwarming story with me. He was truly loved by so many people and I do not think he had a single enemy. He had a beautiful way of getting along with everyone and bringing people together. Dad also had an incredibly easy-going way about him and this naturally drew people to him.

He also had an incredible work ethic. Growing up I always thought we had a lot of money because we had the largest house on the street, a swimming pool, and we attended private school. This wasn't really the case. It was not until I was older that I realized the incredible sacrifice that both my parents made for us to grow up with everything that we had.

My father was a heavy equipment operator who decided to open his own excavating company late in life called

Connecticut Excavating. He was also known in the construction industry as "Gradall Pete" because at one point, he had three Gradalls. For those that are not familiar with them, they are huge machines that look similar to large cranes. When I was having pool parties and he would come home with one of those things, everyone would scatter!

Looking back on it, this must have been an enormous risk that he took to open this business so late in his career with five kids at home, but he succeeded. At the time, none of this meant anything to me, but now I certainly have a great appreciation and respect for everything that he accomplished. Most importantly, he was a devout Christian, a great father, friend, and human being. I miss having him here on this earth, but so look forward to being with him again in Heaven.

Contents

Contents

Acknowledgments

First, I would like to thank my Lord and Savior Jesus Christ who means everything to me.

The leadership team at Banyan Treatment Center, for the opportunity to share God's word to our clients on a daily basis, and for providing a platform for God's transforming power to be on display for our clients and staff.

My sisters Lisa Turcotte and Bonnie Acampora, the two most supportive people who stood by me during the worst times in my life—and there were many of those.

My amazing editor and friend, Tamlynn Rubin, whose combined passion and talent are second to none.

The awesome team of professionals at Wipf and Stock Publishers.

My two best friends whom I have known for many years, Rob Kauffman and Jordan Berk, who are among very few people that share my sense of humor.

My brother-in-law, Mario Turcotte, who has helped me in so many areas of my life, and Adriana Aycart-Ospina, a really close, trustworthy friend.

Paula LaRocca, who has been a great asset to the writing of this book.

Introduction

IT IS SUCH AN incredible blessing to begin writing my second book here in the mountains of Santa Fe, New Mexico. Prior to my relationship with God, my life revolved around advancing my career in the corporate security industry, making money, drinking, and having a worldly good time. I was living out the saying, "work hard play hard." This lifestyle escalated when I began working in the difficult and competitive environment of New York City. My interaction with God was limited to being a "CEO Christian," meaning "Christmas and Easter Only," and I basically responded to adversity from an emotional standpoint, seldom considering the effect my response, or lack of response, would have on others. Since becoming a Christian who is now working in ministry, I have faced many situations in which I might have responded as I did in the past, but since then I have developed a moral compass and an anchor for my soul. I have the word of God, the Bible. I now apply it to the challenges I face with much different outcomes. You can do the same if you began to apply Biblical truth to your life.

By no means am I perfect in the areas referenced in this book, as all of us are simply a work in progress. However, through prayer and meditating on His word, He gave me the strength to overcome many issues. This could not have happened through my own strength. One of the reasons I am sharing these short stories is the hope that others would be empowered to apply this practice to their own lives, by allowing faith in God, and His word, to overcome the emotionally charged obstacles life throws our way. To put these principles into context and provide some background on me, here is some of my story.

I grew up in Connecticut in a typical middle class neighborhood. We were Roman Catholic Italians. As some of you may imagine, I attended Catholic school and served as an altar boy. We were expected to attend church on Saturday night or Sunday. This was not stressed as much by my mother, as by my father. I was an okay student but constantly in trouble.

As I grew into adulthood, I continued to experience many trials and tribulations primarily due to the fact that I had never applied any faith-based principles to my daily life. I knew of God but I had no relationship with Him. I never really understood the intimate notion of a personal relationship with Jesus Christ until a Sunday service many years later. I was at Calvary Chapel in Fort Lauderdale when I accepted Him as my Lord and Savior. That is when I began my journey of knowing of Him.

Chapter 1

A Matter of the Heart

When I look back on my life and see how God has brought me from the depths of despair to now having such a close relationship with Him, it truly amazes me what unconditional love He has for us. I have been journaling on a daily basis for the past seven years, and when I moved back to Florida I noticed two journals in the trunk of my car. I knew the contents were from a period of my life that was filled with tremendous pain, so I avoided them for a long time. Finally one day I brought them in and opened them up. To my surprise it was incredibly encouraging to see just how many times God had shown up in my life, and how many prayers He had answered. I was blessed to read how some of those specific prayers had come to fruition in my life today.

One prayer in particular was to be able to share God's word with those who are broken and suffering and to be able to draw from my experiences in helping others who are also suffering. God had turned my pain into an incredible opportunity to bless others. In my previous career compassion was not a big part of the job. In fact it hindered my ability to do the job effectively. Back then my job was basically to have people fired, arrested, or both, when dealing with theft, fraud, and embezzlement cases. It was easy to avoid having compassion for these people. They were hurting the company and often times other employees. However, when it came to the policy violations and having to address the minor offenses, having a heart could get in the way. Consequently I became desensitized to human suffering. I had to focus directly on the infraction, not on the emotional pain of the troubled person in each situation.

To shed more light on my perspective, in 2003 I was promoted to director of security for a large retail company and moved to northern California. I had moved up the ranks in New York City, one of the most brutal political environments that I had ever encountered. After long winters in New York, the west coast was a welcome change of climate. Between the scenic environment, the professionalism, and the laid back nature of these very competent people, life was good. Unfortunately about a year later I found myself in the middle of a corporate political war. During this time I became very anxious and was totally stressed out. A friend suggested that I see a doctor who prescribed Xanax, the anti-anxiety drug. It made me calmer and I felt more relaxed. In a strange way, it worked too well. I began taking more and more, and began drinking to excess. I experienced the law of diminishing returns first-hand, that is, the more I took the more I needed to sustain a calm state. It was a vicious cycle that eventually led to an even bigger issue with gambling.

When you are in a dark place, dealing with depression, anxiety, betrayal, resentments, and unforgiveness, you look for relief from wherever you can find it. At that time, the casino life seemed like an answer to all my problems and a great escape from a dark reality. I spent so much money that I became a high-limit player and was treated like a VIP, with perks that included presidential suites, concert tickets, and all the alcohol I could drink for free. It was a perfect storm because I had made large amounts of money via stock options in my company, and now I had a place to go to escape from my pain as well as resources to fuel my new obsession. The substantial monetary losses took a dramatic toll on me both financially and spiritually.

I never thought the pain and suffering that I endured over those seven years would be used by God to move me to where I am today. My sister Lisa always said God had a plan for my life and that He would use my suffering for good, but at the time it fell on deaf ears. God does in fact work all things together for good. He uses our pain for good and he is close to us when we are at our lowest. It is difficult to grasp that when we are trapped in the storms of life, but it is Truth. If you are in a storm right now, I encourage you to cry out to God from the deepest part of your being, surrender your will to His will, and begin to trust Him with all of your heart. He will show up in your life to restore all that was lost, and you will then begin the journey of allowing God to transform you from the inside out.

Bible Verse: Trust in the Lord with all your heart, And lean not on your own understanding; In all your ways acknowledge Him, And He shall direct your paths.—Proverbs 3:5–6, NKJV

Overcoming Emotional Obstacles through Faith

Heavenly Father, I know that Your ways are better than mine, because You are the Creator of all things, and that You love me and know what is best for me. Help me to always seek Your wisdom, and to trust You to guide me all the days of my life. In Jesus' name I pray, Amen.

Chapter 2

Be Anxious for Nothing . . .

PHILIPPIANS 4:6–7 READS, "BE anxious for nothing, but in everything by prayer and supplication, with thanksgiving, let your requests be made known to God; and the peace of God, which surpasses all understanding, will guard your hearts and minds through Christ Jesus" (NKJV).

These two verses have a deep significance to me. For a period of time, I was suffering with crippling anxiety. It initially started due to unforgiveness and at times it became so bad that my legs would become numb, making it difficult to walk, concentrate, or think clearly. I suddenly became inundated with Christians giving me this verse because it begins with, "Be anxious for nothing." I must have read it one hundred times, and many of those times I actually became more anxious about the fact that I was even in a position such that people felt the need to give me this verse. I also became more anxious because it was not helping me to feel better when I read it. I would think to myself, "If this doesn't work, and all of these holy people were so sure that it would, then nothing will!" The other thing that really infuriated me was the comment from Christians saying those four dreaded words, "Where is your faith?" It was almost as if the words flowed out of their mouths in slow motion. Let me give some friendly side advice to people who want to encourage someone suffering with anxiety or depression. Please don't make comments questioning that individual's faith or minimize what they are going through! That might make them actually shut down and run away from the faith. Most comments are well intended but unless you have dealt with the same struggles, it is difficult to really understand.

I had read that verse from Philippians many times with no relief when I finally realized why. The bottom line was that I had never actually done what the verse instructed. "Let your requests be made know to God." I was not *doing* that; I was only *reading* the words over, and over. James 1:22 tells us, "Be doers of the word, and not hearers only, deceiving yourselves" (NKJV). For example, if someone gave you a book on losing weight, but all you did was read it without following what it says to do, you obviously wouldn't have any positive results. Imagine that the person who gave it to you later asked you about your weight, and you had to confess that you actually gained ten pounds! In a similar way this is what many of us do with the Bible. Some can quote it from Genesis to Revelation but they don't actually apply it to their lives. For quite some time after I first came to know the Lord, I know I didn't. It took me a long time, but when I finally began to actually apply what I read in scripture, things began to change for the better. I began asking God for His peace, the peace that surpasses all understanding. Although I am still a work in progress, I am striving to be more Christ-like each day. The progress I have made is only due to obedience in following God's word. This is at the heart of this book—applying biblical truths to your life.

Bible Verse: Be anxious for nothing, but in everything by prayer and supplication, with thanksgiving, let your requests be made known to God; and the peace of God, which surpasses all understanding, will guard your hearts and minds through Christ Jesus.—Philippians 4:6–7, NKJV

Heavenly Father, You are the Provider of my peace. Help me to walk in obedience to your word and do Your will, not my own. I ask for a continual overflow of Your peace in my life, the peace that surpasses all understanding. In Jesus' name I pray, Amen.

Chapter 3

A Deeper Relationship with God

IF YOU HAVE BEEN in faith circles for any length of time you have probably heard the phrase, "You need a relationship with God." If you are like me, you may have questioned what that even means and how you could have a relationship with someone you cannot even see. As it is, I sometimes have a difficult enough time having relationships with people I *can* see!

One of the illustrations I use with the clients in the Faith in Recovery Program is to think of anyone with whom you have a solid rapport and ask yourself how did you get to that place? What was it that transpired? What was the process that took place for this to develop?

You probably spent more time with that person, you confided in them, and they in you. Over time you developed a mutual trust with that person; they know everything about you and they are completely transparent with you about themselves. In the same way, we need to do those things with our Heavenly Father. We need to seek Him with all of our hearts, not just when we are in a bad situation or when an emergency occurs. That is not what God wants from us.

To develop this relationship with God through Christ, we need to spend more time with Him in prayer, meditate on His word, listen to music with lyrics that glorify Him, and pursue Him. In Hebrews 11:6 it says, "But without faith it is impossible to please Him, for he who comes to God must believe that He is, and that He is a rewarder of those who diligently seek Him" (NKJV).

Therefore, I say seek and pursue Him. Learn as much as you can about Him. One of my favorite verses is Jeremiah 29:11–13, "'For I know the plans I have for you,' declares the Lord, 'plans to prosper you and not to harm you, plans to give you hope and a future. Then you will call on me and come and pray to me, and I will listen to you. You will seek me and find me when you seek me with all your heart'" (NIV). Did you catch that last line, about seeking Him with all of your heart? I cannot stress the importance of that enough.

In the past, I was guilty of using God as a spare tire for emergencies only, calling on Him only when something was wrong. It is kind of like that person who only calls you or shows up when they need something. That is not a real relationship; it is more like that person is just using you when they need something. Yet we sometimes treat the Creator of the universe that way. Think of it this way, God should be the steering wheel directing and guiding us, not a spare tire only called on for an emergency. Contrary to the bumper sticker stating, "God is my co-pilot," nothing can be further from the truth! We are in the passenger seat and He is driving. When we take the wheel we usually end up lost in life. For a long time I know I was, but now I am found. I was spiritually blind, but now I see! I put all my trust in Him because He is worthy of our trust and praise.

A great model of a relationship with God is seen in King David, particularly in the psalms that he wrote. David was not perfect by any means, and he fell short at times, like all of us. He made some really poor choices, such as committing adultery with Bathsheba, and even worse having her husband killed. Trust me, he was no angel. After making these horrible decisions he wrote Psalm 51. Consider verses 1–13:

> "Have mercy on me, O God,
> according to your unfailing love;
> according to your great compassion
> blot out my transgressions.
> Wash away all my iniquity
> and cleanse me from my sin.
> For I know my transgressions,
> and my sin is always before me.
> Against you, you only, have I sinned
> and done what is evil in your sight;
> so you are right in your verdict
> and justified when you judge.
> Surely I was sinful at birth,
> sinful from the time my mother conceived me.
> Yet you desired faithfulness even in the womb;
> you taught me wisdom in that secret place.
> Cleanse me with hyssop, and I will be clean;
> wash me, and I will be whiter than snow.
> Let me hear joy and gladness;
> let the bones you have crushed rejoice.
> Hide your face from my sins
> and blot out all my iniquity.
> Create in me a pure heart, O God,
> and renew a steadfast spirit within me.
> Do not cast me from your presence
> or take your Holy Spirit from me

Restore to me the joy of your salvation
and grant me a willing spirit, to sustain me.
Then I will teach transgressors your ways,
so that sinners will turn back to you" (NIV).

Now that is a good example of transparency and written completely from the heart. It's not surprising that David was known as a man after God's own heart. The reality is that God already knows our sins. It's not as if we are telling Him something of which He is not aware. When you do fall short of the mark and sin, as we all do, I would encourage you to follow David's model: confess it, ask for forgiveness, and move forward. Don't get bogged down with guilt, regret, and shame. Simply move on with appreciation that you have in God an all-powerful, all knowing, and all forgiving Father.

Bible Verse: But from there you will search again for the Lord your God. And if you search for him with all your heart and soul, you will find him.—Deuteronomy 4:29, NLT

Heavenly Father, I know You look at the heart and not outward appearances. Give me the strength to have a heart that is pure. Help me to be more transparent, and completely honest with You and those around me. Search my heart and allow me to see and change all areas that are not pleasing to you. In Jesus' name I pray, Amen.

Chapter 4

Come As You Are

ONE THING THAT WAS drilled into me from a very early age was a sense of guilt. This is not intended as a knock on any specific denomination because I know there is good and bad in all of them. However, in the particular church and school that I attended, it seems that guilt, shame, and money were central themes. That's not to say that God was not also a major focus. I'm writing about this topic because I have come across many clients who enter our Christian substance abuse program at Banyan, who say they grew up going to church, but as they got older at some point they stopped going because of negative emotions associated with their church experience. They typically say their church memories are filled with emotions such as guilt, or it seemed very condemning, as if God was out to get them. They frequently add that they felt judged and felt as if they could never be good enough.

Every time I hear this it takes me right back to exactly how I felt, and as I started to think about it at a deeper level I realized that these are the exact same things that God speaks *against* in His word. Feeling *guilty* at church? "If we confess our sins, He is faithful and just and will forgive us our sins and purify us from all unrighteousness" (1 John 1:9, NIV). God speaking through the prophet Isaiah tells us, "I, even I, am He who blots out your transgressions for My own sake; And I will not remember your sins" (Isaiah 43:25, NKJV). Feeling *condemned* at church? Paul tells us clearly in Romans 8:1–2, "Therefore, there is now no condemnation for those who are in Christ Jesus, because through Christ Jesus the law of the Spirit who gives life has set you free from the law of sin and death" (NIV). Feeling *judged* at church? At the Sermon on the Mount, Jesus said, "Do not judge others, and you will not be judged. For you will be treated as you treat others. The standard you use in judging is the standard by which you will be judged" (Matthew 7:1–2, NLT). As we see, there are numerous verses in the Bible where we learn that, guilt, condemnation, and judgment are not what our loving Father God intends for us.

To summarize, we have Apostle Paul telling us there is no condemnation for those who are in Christ (the believers in Christ); Jesus telling us not to judge; and the Apostle John telling us that if we confess, God will forgive us of our sins. God Himself tells us through the prophet Isaiah that He will not even remember our sins. If you are new to the Bible or unaware of these verses, I would encourage you to meditate on them and allow them to really sink in to your spirit. I would also encourage you to find a good Bible-based church that teaches sound doctrine because the teaching that you may have been exposed to may have been contrary to the teachings of Christ.

If there were no forgiveness through Christ, there would have been no gospel of Matthew because before Jesus asked him to be one of his disciples he had been a crooked tax collector for the oppressive Romans. There would be no Apostle Paul either because, prior to his encounter with the risen Christ on the road to Damascus, he had once been a persecutor of the early church. I am hoping you see a pattern here. God is a merciful and loving Father who offers us forgiveness through Christ. If we allow Him to work in our lives, He will make us a new creation in Christ, and turn our mess into our message.

However, it is important to understand that God is not going to do everything we want Him to do, but He will often do the things we cannot do by working behind the scenes on our behalf. Often times He may set up divine encounters, soften the heart of that prospective employer on the other side of the desk, or give you just the right words to say to someone who is broken in spirit. If we put all of our trust in Him, we only need to do the things we are able to do, and He will do the rest.

As for guilt, judgment, and condemnation, picture those words in big bold print on hundreds of files in your mind for all the times you have felt those emotions, and hit the delete button. As we have seen, there are multiple Bible verses that explain God's position on these topics. Move forward and receive all of the incredible blessings God has planned for you.

Bible Verse: Then Jesus said, "Come to me, all of you who are weary and carry heavy burdens, and I will give you rest."—Matthew 11:28, NLT

Heavenly Father, Allow me to better see people through Your eyes and not my own. Help me to be free of judgmental

opinions of others. Instead, help me to be an encouragement to others, especially those who are suffering and
broken in spirit. I don't always know who those people are,
but You do, and You understand their pain. Allow me to
have a more compassionate heart for others. Free me from
the emotions of guilt, condemnation, or feeling judged by
others, and help me to embrace Your loving forgiveness. In
Jesus' name I pray, Amen.

Chapter 5

First Remove the Plank from Your Own Eye . . .

ONE AREA IN WHICH God has really given me a wake-up call involves judging others. I can think of a related situation that involved Rick Warren, the popular pastor who founded *Saddleback Church*, a Christian evangelical mega church in Lakewood, California. He is also a well-known author of numerous Christian books, including bestseller, *The Purpose Driven Life*, as well as others. Like many people, despite a very busy schedule, I still manage to keep up with social media. For a period of time, I came across several not-so-complimentary posts about Pastor Warren. Obviously, this is not uncommon with any public figure. Details aside, let's just say that many of these posts were simply gossip.

However, during this time I began to believe some of these posts and found myself judging him based on what some obscure person on social media would post. Around the same time, I attended a faith conference in Nashville, Tennessee where I found myself at an incredible service featuring Christian singer/songwriter Michael W. Smith and Pastor Warren. First, Smith's worship performance was absolutely amazing! Next, Rick Warren spoke and shared the story of how he had recently lost his son to suicide. It was one of the most powerful and moving stories I have ever heard, and completely from the heart. At one point Rick became very emotional, and Michael began to play the song *Worthy is the Lamb*. Even though Rick attempted to use his hands to cover his face, it was still obvious that he was visibly weeping. As the song played, and during most of the time he was sharing the story, I felt the most incredible conviction from the Holy Spirit about judging this man. I had never felt so strongly convicted, and I remember asking God for forgiveness for judging him, and for the strength to never judge anyone again!

This story illustrates how we can never be certain of what another person is going through, hence it is not our place to cast judgment upon others. We must first recognize our own flaws and ask God to help us avoid having a critical spirit. There is only one true judge who sees the heart of everyone and He is our Creator.

Bible Verse: Judge not, that you be not judged. For with what judgment you judge, you will be judged; and with the measure you use, it will be measured back to you. And why do you look at the speck in your brother's eye, but do not consider the plank in your own eye? Or how can you say to your brother, 'Let me remove the speck from your eye'; and 'look, a plank is in your own eye?' Hypocrite! First remove the plank from your own eye, and then you will see clearly to remove the speck from your brother's eye.—Matthew 7:15, NKJV

Overcoming Emotional Obstacles through Faith

Heavenly Father, You clearly state in Your word not to judge others, yet I still sometimes fall into this trap. Please provide me with the strength to overcome any areas of judgment in my life. In Jesus' name I pray, Amen.

Chapter 6

I'm OK—You're Not

This title is a play on words from the book entitled, *I'M OK—YOU'RE O.K.*[1] If you knew my sense of humor you would probably think it sounds like something I would say. I think it's pretty funny, especially if you tell someone jokingly that it is the title of a book by a mutual friend who is very self-absorbed. That is my sense of humor in a nutshell. My brand of humor is similar to Saturday Night Live from the nineties, when the cast was full of amazing talents such as Phil Hartman, Dana Carvey, and Chris Farley.

The next two stories will continue our focus on the topic of judging others. As I mentioned earlier, I attend Calvary Chapel in Fort Lauderdale. At my church, there is an incredible restaurant that serves delicious food. Due to the fact that it is on the church campus, they are not required to collect sales tax on meals. Side note, for my fellow cheap guys out there, this is a great place to bring a date! I think it is safe to say we have all encountered someone who for whatever reason gets under our skin, so to speak, (you may actually be married to this person). For me, one of these

1. Harris, Thomas A. *I'm OK—You're OK*. Harper Row, 1973.

people happened to be a guy who would often come into the church restaurant and sit near me. He was a bit loud and I just found him annoying. Clearly, I was judging him, without knowing him at all. One night in particular, he again happened to be sitting near me, and my negative perception of him reached an all-time high.

After dinner I went into the sanctuary for the church service. Who do you think I saw speak at the pulpit? It was none other than the loud guy! As it turned out, he was a staff member at another Calvary location. He preached a very powerful message that evening, some of which was on the topic of judging others. Imagine my shock. It was one of the most inspiring lessons I had ever heard at church, and I felt the conviction of the Holy Spirit for judging him throughout his message. A couple of weeks later, I saw him in the sanctuary and could not help but to go up to him and share about how his message had profoundly affected me. I also told him that I had posted about it on social media. He responded in such a humble way, with a big smile, told me that he was aware of my post, and thanked me for my kind words.

What can we learn from this true story? Let's relate it to your life. How many times have you judged someone about something, only to be proven completely wrong? I know I have done so on many occasions. Maybe there are some specific situations that really hit home with you from your past. Reflect on these, and how you felt after finding out you had wrongly judged someone. I would encourage you to try and recall such past situations the next time you start to judge someone. It may just remove your desire to judge others.

This next true story regarding judging others is close to my heart. About five years ago I found myself on social media debating pit bull lovers regarding recent attacks. I remember one heated exchange in particular where I had made a post arguing that there should be a national ban on all pit bulls, and they should all be put down. I had never owned one, nor did I know much about the breed. I simply based my strong opinion on various news reports and idle chats that reported many horrible incidents involving them and their aggression. Fast forward about four years later, to 2016. I received a call from a family member about an abandoned dog that needed a home. I had no idea what kind of dog it was, but she was really feeling bad for this pup so I stopped by to check him out. He was so dirty from being on the street that she had to give him several baths to get him back to his normal color.

When I met him, he was a bit thin and anxious, and possibly wondering what his fate would be. Who could blame him? I took him home with me, and that first night he went to sleep on the couch. The next morning I awoke to his cold nose on my arm nudging me to wake up. That day I took him to the vet and found out the he had a double ear infection and was under weight. The vet confirmed that he was a blue nose American pit bull terrier. He was about two years old. The vet was a big pit bull fan and owner of two precious pit bulls himself. He really took a liking to the dog. I had to give him a name for the official paperwork. It was kind of exciting as if I was adopting a child. During the process he would look at me with such sweet, innocent eyes, (the dog, not the vet). It dawned on me that I was now responsible for this beautiful animal that would later become a best friend. I pondered what to name him. What else other than a biblical name, right? I named him Luke, after the author of the gospel of the same name. On our way home from the vet it was as if "Luke the Dog" and I bonded in some way. I think he realized I was not going to hurt him, but instead give him the love and affection that he had probably never received.

From that point on, Luke has never left my side. We run and walk together in the mornings and evenings. He loves car rides and he typically sticks his head out through the sunroof, with a huge smile on his face, and dribbles slobber down my arm. For some strange reason that does not bother me, nor do the vet bills, or even when he eats my shoes. We have the best of times walking on the beach, going to the dog park, and visiting his favorite pet store. Our days are not complete without an evening wrestling match. When I bring him in to the office, he always puts a smile on the faces of our clients and staff at Banyan Treatment Center's Faith in Recovery Program, where I work.

One of the many things that surprised me was how people in the neighborhood received him. Almost everyone we encounter really likes him. They ask to pet him, ask various questions about him, and on several occasions people have even asked to breed him with their pit bull as they proudly show me pictures of their dogs.

I have since conducted a lot of research on pit bulls and I have been astonished to learn that according to the American Temperament Test Society, since they started testing dogs in 1977, 87.4% of pit bulls tested have passed their comprehensive temperament test.[2]

How did we get to where we are today in the United States with the American pit bull terrier at the top of many of the "most dangerous" dog charts, and with many counties and cities throughout the country banning them? As I mentioned previously, I was someone who once believed the lie that all pit bulls are vicious. Since becoming a proud owner of one, I can say with confidence that I believe pit

2. American Temperament Test Society, Inc. https://atts.org/breed-statistics/statistics-page1/

bulls are by no means inherently vicious. If they are aggressive, then they were likely manipulated by people who have no business being around dogs. American pit bull terriers can be incredible companions who love people, including children. They would naturally much rather be chasing a ball, running for a Frisbee, or cuddling with you on the couch, rather than fighting other dogs. Yes, they are very strong, agile, and tenacious, but they generally have to be mistreated and manipulated by people to become the vicious dogs that we hear about on the news. They are known for being incredibly loyal to their owners, and people with evil intentions often take advantage of the pit bull's strong desire to please by exploiting this trait. It is extremely disturbing to me when people take advantage of this wonderful creation of God. I read an interesting article by Eastown Veterinary Clinic that I think sums it up pretty well, "Prior to 1980, horror stories about pit bull attacks were almost non-existent. In the eighties, we saw a resurgence in two things: drugs and dog-fighting . . . Many of the issues and stories that are publicized about pit bulls are not the fault of the breed itself, but rather the way individual dogs have been inhumanely and maliciously raised."[3]

Bible Verse: So in everything, do to others what you would have them do to you, for this sums up the Law and the Prophets.—Matthew 7:12, NIV

3. Eastown Veterinary Clinic. https://www.eastownvet.com/happy-pit-bull-appreciation-month-heres-what-you-need-to-know-about-pitties/

Heavenly Father, Search my heart and show me anywhere in me that does not reflect Your image. Continue to strengthen my resolve to avoid judging others. Allow me to follow Your commandment to love my neighbor as myself. In Jesus' name I pray, Amen.

Chapter 7

Learning to Forgive by Practicing Forgiveness

NOT SO LONG AGO, I faced a challenging situation when a person that I had been involved with in a business arrangement became bitter and resentful because I decided not to continue to do business with him. In this particular case, the business relationship had run its course. Without giving too much detail, let's just say I felt it was time to move on and pursue new partnerships. My previous associate went out of his way to interfere with my new business partners in numerous ways that put them in a very difficult position. In fact, they were entirely disgusted with his behaviors, and we all agreed that his tactics were both unfair and unprofessional.

When I saw how upset my new partners had become, this fueled my anger and my mind raced through numerous ways I could retaliate. Maybe you find yourself in a similar situation where you know you were wronged and others confirm it? How do we respond as Christians? If this had occurred prior to when I became a Christian, and had

I not consulted the word of God, my response would not have been positive or appropriate.

The results would most likely have been a prolonged political battle against my former associate, filled with tremendous stress, anxiety, and anger for me, as well as for many other people involved. However, before starting a conflict, almost begrudgingly, I sought out what the Bible had to say on the matter and came across the verse that begins, "Never pay back evil with more evil . . . " (Romans 12:17, NLT).

I must have read this at least 25 times over the next few days. I had to allow this truth to resonate in my spirit, not just in my head. I had to allow God to transform me by changing the way I thought and responded to situations that would typically provoke my anger and other emotions.

I had worked in Manhattan for six years, and after the first few months I realized that I would have to learn to retaliate or defend myself as most people did, otherwise I wouldn't be able to survive there for long. Having grown up in New England, this way of responding was very foreign to me. However, after a few months I began to master the art of Manhattan work politics in all its fullness.

Nevertheless, I had since become a new creation in Christ and after reading the next few verses from Romans, and a lot of prayer, I was finally able to actually forgive instead of retaliate. I encourage you to take this bit of advice and allow God's word to penetrate your natural, fleshly response to get even. Instead, learn to forgive when you are wronged. Not only does God command us to forgive one another in scripture, but also once you do so, you will find that you have peace of mind instead of inner turmoil. If you struggle with unforgiveness, or find yourself miserable from holding grudges, I am convinced that whether you are a Bible reading Christian, or even if you have never picked up a Bible, this verse can have a major positive impact on your life!

Bible Verse: Never pay back evil with more evil. Do things in such a way that everyone can see that you are honorable. Do all that you can to live in peace with everyone. Dear friends, never take revenge. Leave that to the righteous anger of God.—Romans 12:17–19, NLT

Heavenly Father, I come to You, seeking the strength to apply what Your word says about forgiveness. Help me to let go of past hurts that destroy my peace. Heal me from past wounds that prevent me from forgiving others. Let me be at peace with anyone who has wronged me. In Jesus' name I pray, Amen.

Chapter 8

God's Transforming Power

On March 6, 2005, I accepted Jesus Christ as my Lord and Savior at Calvary Chapel, Fort Lauderdale. I will never forget that day. I was so focused on the biblical message of the service, that I still remember some of it today. Growing up, I attended many church services, but none of them had ever had such a profound impact on me. The pastor had made three altar calls at the end of the service, and was making a fourth. At the time, I did not really even understand what an altar call was, I just knew in the deepest part of my being that I needed to be up there at the altar, and I needed to get right with God. I went up front filled with a lot of resentments, anger, Xanax, and a glimmer of hope. I recited the sinner's prayer and next I was ushered to the room for new believers. I sensed change, however, I was not really sure what was happening.

The next night I literally felt the incredible presence of the Holy Spirit. It was 10:14pm, and I was on the phone with a close friend from California. The best way to describe it would be to imagine yourself sitting outside in freezing cold air at the ocean's edge, when suddenly a wave of warmth comes over you like a cleansing, purifying water, filled with peace, love, and joy. As I experienced His presence, I described it in real time to my friend on the phone. A few minutes later I felt almost as if I had become a totally new person. As Apostle Paul wrote, "Therefore if anyone is in Christ he is a new creation, the old is gone the new has come" (2 Corinthians 5:17, NKJV).

Prior to this experience, I had never heard that verse. However, when I first heard it I knew exactly what Paul was referring to, as I had experienced the transforming power of God.

The next day I was a completely different person. I changed an elderly woman's tire and drove my nephew to visit his friend an hour away at Jackson Memorial Hospital. I could not wait for the next church service! I waited with the anticipation of a child on Christmas Eve. I could not wait to go home and read the Bible. Just 48 hours earlier I would have never done these things. I had been focused solely on myself and wanted little to do with helping others or learning about God. Instead, I began passionately pursuing God and getting involved in numerous faith-based courses, Bible studies, and other church activities. In fact, I was spending so much time at the church that I actually bought a condominium about two blocks away from it. I had been looking to move and figured that since I was there at least five or six days a week, I might as well be as close as possible.

Initially during this time I was trying to understand what had actually occurred with me. After much research on the topic of salvation and conversions, I came across many people who told stories of similar experiences. This is not to say that salvation in Christ will always cause people to feel the same way I did. The Bible clearly states, "We walk by faith not by sight" (2 Corinthians 5:17, NKJV). It is not about a feeling or observing something tangible.

Most people do not have this type of experience. An important point regarding this is found Romans 10:9, "If you declare with your mouth Jesus in Lord and believe in your heart God raised Him from the dead you will be saved" (NIV). That, my friends, is truly amazing grace. I came to learn that if we allow God into our lives, He will transform us from the inside out. To this day, some twelve years later, I am fully convinced that there is neither anyone nor anything on this earth that could have changed my heart, other than our awesome and merciful Lord.

Bible Verse: For God so loved the world that He gave His only begotten Son, that whoever believes in Him should not perish but have everlasting life.—John 3:16, NKJV

Heavenly Father, Your grace, mercy, and love for me are beyond human comprehension. Thank you for allowing me into Your kingdom, and for filling me with Your peace that surpasses all understanding. In Jesus' name I pray, Amen.

Chapter 9

Words Hurt

THE SECOND HALF OF Luke 6:45 tells us, "For out of the abundance of the heart his mouth speaks" (KJV). With this truth in mind it leads me to believe that if something is unresolved and eating at us inside, at some point it will be spoken out of our mouths. I have experienced this when I did not confront an issue or person who was doing or saying things that offended me. When we do not resolve the initial issue, other things get added to it creating a state of unease and overwhelm. Subsequently we may have a negative response to someone because we are still reeling inside from the initial unresolved issue. How do we effectively resolve the underlying conflict to prepare ourselves for the inevitable next difficult situation? In Ephesians 4:15 Apostle Paul says to "speak the truth in love" (NIV). I try to incorporate this into my life by being completely honest when responding to someone who I feel is offending or opposing me, but to also do it in a loving manner. For many of you responding, *in a loving manner*, is the difficult part. It was for me, and still is sometimes, but you will be able to resolve many more conflicts by working to apply this approach in your lives. At first, this will not be easy, especially if you have been suppressing issues for a long time. It will get easier as you ask God for the strength to apply His word to this area of your life and continue to put this practice into action. The alternative to speaking the truth in love is obvious to me. We either say nothing, and the conflict ends up stored inside of us in the "unresolved issues file," only to eventually re-emerge at a later time, or we speak the truth, but in a hostile manner, which almost always compounds the problem.

If you continue to struggle in this area, do not get discouraged! I still struggle with these issues too sometimes! However, I am certainly much more effective now with God's help than I ever was trying to deal with these problems on my own. God knows our hearts and He will help you through all conflicts if you simply ask Him. Continue to seek His help with each issue. He is not sitting back waiting for us to fail in order to judge or condemn us. He is a loving Father who wants to help us overcome all of our problems. However, He will not force himself upon us. He gave us the gift of free will so that we always have a choice in the matter. I encourage you to choose to ask Him for strength and wisdom before responding to someone in a manner that you may later regret. When we respond in a hostile or hurtful way, we are not resolving the problem, we are only adding to it.

Bible Verse: A gentle answer deflects anger but harsh words make tempers flare.—Proverbs 15:1, NLT

Heavenly Father, You are all knowing and all powerful. I ask You for help with the way I respond to adversity and people who upset me. Give me the peace and calmness of spirit to speak the truth in love and resolve every conflict. I cannot even begin to overcome this on my own, but I know that, with You, all things are possible. I trust in You to strengthen me in this area of struggle. In Jesus' name I pray, Amen.

Chapter 10

Have You Asked?

ONE OF THE THINGS I hear most from our clients regarding prayer is that they are comfortable praying for someone else, but they somehow feel uncomfortable asking God for anything for themselves. Maybe it has to do with rejection from an earthly father or perhaps being told not to ask for things when they were growing up. I'm no psychologist, nor do I pretend to be, but I do know what Jesus instructed us to do through God's word, and that is to ask! In Luke 11:9–13 Jesus said, "So I say to you: Ask and it will be given to you; seek and you will find; knock and the door will be opened to you. For everyone who asks receives; the one who seeks finds; and to the one who knocks, the door will be opened. Which of you fathers, if your son asks for a fish, will give him a snake instead? Or if he asks for an egg, will give him a scorpion? If you then, though you are evil, know how to give good gifts to your children, how much more will your Father in heaven give the Holy Spirit to those who ask him!" (NIV).

There you have it. God wants us to make our requests known to Him. James, the half brother of Jesus, teaches us in James 4:2–3, "Yet you don't have what you want because you don't ask God for it. And even when you ask, you don't get it because your motives are all wrong" (NLT).

Many times I deal with people who blame God for the troubles in their lives, yet never ask Him for help in resolving them. If we consider the meanings of ask, seek, and knock, these actions are all forms of initiating interaction with God. It is as if we are standing outside a door and become angry because no one inside lets us in, however, we never even knocked. God is all-knowing and He wants us to initiate the dialogue by deliberate communication with Him through prayer.

Let's take a look at the Sermon on the Mount—some call it the original Bible study. One of the many incredible gifts that come from this passage is the Lord's Prayer. In Matthew 6:5–15 the people ask Jesus how to pray and he responds:

> "And when you pray, you shall not be like the hypocrites. For they love to pray standing in the synagogues and on the corners of the streets, that they may be seen by men. Assuredly, I say to you, they have their reward. But you, when you pray, go into your room, and when you have shut your door, pray to your Father who is in the secret place; and your Father who sees in secret will reward you openly. And when you pray, do not use vain repetitions as the heathen do. For they think that they will be heard for their many words. Therefore do not be like them. For your Father knows the things you have need of before you ask Him. In this manner, therefore, pray:

> Our Father in heaven,
> Hallowed be Your name.
> Your kingdom come.

> Your will be done
>
> On earth as it is in heaven.
>
> Give us this day our daily bread.
>
> And forgive us our debts,
>
> As we forgive our debtors.
>
> And do not lead us into temptation,
>
> But deliver us from the evil one.
>
> For Yours is the kingdom and the power and the glory forever. Amen" (NKJV).

What can we learn from Jesus' response about how to pray? If we break down the Lord's Prayer, the words "Our Father" mean that we should come to God the Father with reverence, honor and praise. "Hallowed be your name" means holy is Your name, or setting Him apart. "Your kingdom come. Your will be done on earth as it is in heaven." This part means we ask not that *our* will be done, but rather that *His* will be done. The next few lines involve asking or making our requests known to Him. When we say, "Give us this day our daily bread," it is a request. "Forgive us our debts." "Do not lead us into temptation." "Deliver us from the evil one." These are all still requests. Finally, we end the prayer with reverence, honor, and praise. "For yours is the kingdom and the power and the glory forever. Amen."

The Lord's Prayer is a model based on the way Jesus instructed us to pray. If half of it is about asking or making our petitions known to God on our own behalf, then why would we ever feel guilty or ashamed to ask God for help in areas of struggle in our lives? Asking God for help is in His will, and consequently if we do not ask then we are actually operating in our own will, not His.

If you struggle with taking action in this area, start out making small requests and ask for things that line up with His will. For example, God's will for us is to forgive others who have wronged us. If we are praying for something that revolves around vengeance or unforgiveness, then it is doubtful He is going to answer such a prayer. Asking God for the strength and grace to forgive others is aligned with His will, and more likely to be answered by Him.

Something else I notice is that people often pray for something such as a job, and then they profess the exact opposite later in conversation. I have witnessed this happen whereby after praying and asking God to bless them with a job, they later express doubt and negativity about God fulfilling that prayer. We need to know that He operates through faith, therefore if we demonstrate a lack of faith we are probably canceling out those prayers. The economy of this world is money, and in a similar way God's economy is faith. Hebrews 11:6 tells us, "But without faith it is impossible to please Him" (NKJV).

In summary, God wants us to ask Him for help, as illustrated in the Lord's Prayer from the Sermon on the Mount. He also operates through faith so we do not want to fall into the pattern of praying for things and then professing the exact opposite. We want to walk fully in faith, believing that He will provide.

As a final point on the Lord's Prayer, we first begin the prayer with, "Your will be done," and next we make our requests. He may not answer our prayers as quickly as we would like, but we must keep in mind that faith in God includes faith in His will and this includes faith in His timing as part of that will.

Bible Verse: Ask and it will be given to you; seek and you will find; knock and the door will be opened to you.— Mathew 7:7, NIV

Overcoming Emotional Obstacles through Faith

Heavenly Father, You say in Your word to ask, seek, and knock. I have decided to put my trust in You and Your word. Please help me to not follow my own will when trouble comes, but instead to put all my trust in You and Your divine will for my life. In Jesus' name I pray, Amen.

Chapter 11

You Are Not a Doormat

WE HAVE ALL HEARD the term, "doormat," used to describe people who allow others to walk all over them. They might be described as pushovers, or people who are manipulated and frequently mocked for not standing up for themselves. I struggled with wanting to avoid this label when I first became a Christian. How do I respond to confrontation or manipulation now that I am a follower of Christ? What is the protocol for conflict resolution now? I was in unfamiliar waters. I learned that, contrary to popular belief, Jesus was not a doormat or a pushover, and He was definitely never manipulated. At every turn He did not hesitate to confront the Jewish leaders, Pharisees, or Scribes, even with the knowledge that they were continuously looking for reasons to trap him and kill Him.

In Matthew 10:16, Jesus said this to his disciples, "Behold, I send you out as sheep in the midst of wolves. Therefore be wise as serpents and harmless as doves" (NKJV). What does this verse mean and how can we apply it to our lives today? The sheep reference symbolizes animals that are defenseless and rely completely on their shepherd.

Wolves, the opposite of sheep, are strong predators that can be vicious. In this same way, we as Christians (sheep) are in a world of wolves. Therefore being wise as a serpent would mean we are not to allow others to take advantage of us, and we need to stand on God's truth and be bold in His power. We need to be able to discern evil in all its ways. Being harmless as doves means we must not respond in an evil manner when we discover someone is out to harm us. We must not retaliate, take revenge, or harbor resentments. We now rise above this type of lowly behavior. This may have been our old way of responding, as it was for me, but we are now a new person in Christ! Apostle Paul advises us in 1 Corinthians 13:11, "When I was a child, I talked like a child, I thought like a child, I reasoned like a child. When I became a man, I put the ways of childhood behind me" (NIV). This means we must rise above old ways of thinking and learn to forgive by practicing forgiveness. Perhaps try looking at it from another perspective. You may have heard the saying that hurting people hurt people. With that in mind, you might want to consider the possibility that people who come against you are actually reacting to their own deep, unresolved wounds. Maybe they are simply crying out for help? Maybe they are in desperate need of compassion, and maybe God wants to use you as the one who provides it! Look at them through the eyes of our Father God. Maybe you can change the story's ending to, "I was able to rise above it all and made a profound difference in a hurting person's life."

Bible Verse: If any of you lacks wisdom, let him ask of God, who gives to all liberally and without reproach, and it will be given to him. But let him ask in faith, with no doubting, for he who doubts is like a wave of the sea driven and tossed by the wind.—James 1:5–6, NKJV

Heavenly Father, I ask for wisdom and compassion in dealing with those who come against me and those who are in need of encouragement. Allow me to be an instrument of your mercy and peace. In Jesus' name I pray, Amen.

Chapter 12

Finding His Peace

FOR A PERIOD OF time in my past I suffered with depression and anxiety. If you have ever dealt with this you may have had people tell you that you need to be grateful for your blessings, or that you need to volunteer to help others to feel better. Honestly, when I would hear that it went in one ear and out the other. It meant nothing to me and only frustrated me when people said it. I understand that in theory it makes sense to tell someone who is suffering with depression those things, but when you are completely broken in spirit and in such an emotionally dark place as I was, those words provide little comfort. However, there is a comforter out there for you who provides restoration, healing, and peace, and His name is Jesus!

Jesus said to his disciples in John 14:27, "Peace I leave with you, My peace I give to you; not as the world gives do I give to you. Let not your heart be troubled, neither let it be afraid" (NKJV). Growing up in the Catholic Church I heard this spoken hundreds of times just before we had to shake hands with the people seated around us prior to communion. "Peace I leave with you, my peace I give to you." I never really gave it much thought until years later when I found myself desperately searching for peace.

Jesus made it very clear that His peace was different from the so-called peace found in the world. This use of the term "*the world*" refers to the worldly system we live in, primarily consisting of material things, and including things such as money, status, position, and worldly power.

Back in 2004 I was director of security for a large California based company and I had all of those things. However, that was the worst year of my life, filled with constant political battles, corporate backstabbing, betrayals, and other conflicts. The material things of the world did nothing to overshadow the inner and outer turmoil that I faced daily. I believe this is why many people who achieve great things from a worldly perspective end up depressed, addicted, or worse. It happens because they believe the same lie that I believed, which is that once you achieve a certain level of success, you will have peace and happiness. This is simply not the case. I'm living proof of this fact, just like many others who were much more successful than me. The world simply cannot provide us with the peace that we desire. Unfortunately many of us had to learn this lesson the hard way.

You may have heard the phrase, "we are all created with a God shaped hole in us." This means that we all have a neediness inside and regardless of what we try to fill that hole with—things such as money, status, position, drugs, or material things—we still are empty until we began to fill this void with God. It would seem logical to assume that having a great many achievements in life will bring us inner peace. However, often when we reach that milestone we still feel empty. Once there, we may look at life and realize that if all our success didn't give us peace, then nothing will. That is the beginning of an emotional slide from the mountaintop down to the pit of despair. The amazing thing is that God is always right there waiting for us, never leaving us nor forsaking us!

We sometimes look at a supernatural God through natural eyes and we "put God in a box," meaning we compare how God will react to how people may have responded to us in the past and we limit Him to human standards. For example, if you hurt someone, you might think they will forgive you, once or possibly even twice. That's about it; surely no one would forgive you after you let them down three times. Yet here we have the Creator of the universe and mankind, whom we have we rejected countless times, and still He welcomes us back and forgives us! It is truly amazing when you think about it. Seeking peace in the things of this world is like running east looking for a sunset. It's not that God does not want to bless us with wonderful things, He just does not want us to put things of the world before Him. Such things can be gone in the blink of an eye, but God will never desert us.

I fell into this same pattern and I want you to know that true peace is found in the Prince of Peace, Jesus Christ. If you do not already have a relationship with Christ, I encourage you take a leap of faith right now and simply talk to Him and ask Him to come into your life and forgive you of your sins. Ask him to be your Lord, your Savior, and your friend. If you do this, I can assure you it will be the best decision you will ever make in your life.

Bible Verse: The righteous cry out, and the Lord hears them; he delivers them from all their troubles. The Lord is close to the brokenhearted and saves those who are crushed in spirit.—Psalm 34:17–18, NIV

Heavenly Father, I know that confusion does not come from You, so I stand firm on the truth of Your word and I ask for an overflow of Your supernatural peace to come upon me now. I thank You for all that You have done for me. In Jesus' name I pray, Amen.

Chapter 13

Sin Is Crouching at Your Door

MANY PEOPLE HAVE HEARD the Biblical story of Cain and Abel. If you are not familiar with it, hopefully you will have a better understanding of it by the end of this chapter. Cain and Abel were the sons of Adam and Eve. Even though they were brothers, we see just how different they were as we read Genesis 4:2–9:

> " . . . Now Abel kept flocks, and Cain worked the soil. In the course of time Cain brought some of the fruits of the soil as an offering to the Lord. And Abel also brought an offering—fat portions from some of the firstborn of his flock. The Lord looked with favor on Abel and his offering, but on Cain and his offering he did not look with favor. So Cain was very angry, and his face was downcast.
>
> Then the Lord said to Cain, 'Why are you angry? Why is your face downcast? If you do what is right, will you not be accepted? But if you do not do what is right, sin is crouching at your door; it desires to have you, but you must rule over it.' Now Cain said to his brother Abel,

'Let's go out to the field.' While they were in the
field, Cain attacked his brother Abel and killed
him. Then the Lord said to Cain, 'Where is your
brother Abel?' 'I don't know,' he replied. 'Am I
my brother's keeper?'" (NIV).

Whenever I read this story I wonder if Cain was angry
with himself due to his poor choice of an offering, or was
he angrier with God for not looking with favor on his offering? I believe it's the latter. However, Cain was responsible
for his own situation because he completely disregarded
God's clear warning that he needed to get a handle on his
anger when He told him sin was right at his doorstep. God
wanted him to understand that the situation could easily
escalate unless he made effort to control his anger before it
controlled him. Obviously Cain did not heed the warning
and went out and killed his brother.

In summary, Cain brings the wrong offering, becomes
angry with God and his brother, completely disregards what
God tells him about getting his anger in check, kills his
brother, and lies to God about his brother's whereabouts.
The icing on the cake is the disrespectful way he responds
to God after the lie ("Am I my brother's keeper?"). You may
remember that line from the 1991 movie New Jack City but
it actually originated from this exchange between God and
Cain.

Let's fast forward to the here and now in your life, how
many times have you fallen into a similar set of progressive
circumstances where you make a poor choice, get angry
with God, allow the anger to consume you, and this leads
to an outburst of anger, possibly even with an innocent by-
stander caught in the crossfire? You may have made some
poor choices, but rather than focus on a solution, you may
have lashed out at someone else . . . maybe even at God. I
spent many years doing just that prior to getting to know

Christ. However, I realized that this type of behavior is exactly what the crouching enemy wants us to do because of all the negative effects that it generates in our daily lives. It is completely emotionally draining, it is time consuming, it hurts others, and in turn it ultimately hurts us.

Apostle Paul in Ephesians 4:26 writes, "In your anger do not sin . . . Do not let the sun go down while you are still angry" (NIV). Paul is exhorting us to resolve our issues in the same day they occur, before the sun goes down. As you may have experienced, the more time goes by after an unresolved conflict, the more difficult it becomes to forgive. While I would not recommend responding in the heat of the moment, it should definitely be at some point the same day.

At this point I believe it is worthwhile to list five suggestions regarding anger and how to address the person with whom you have a conflict:

1. Take some time to calm down before speaking to the person you feel has upset you.

2. Reflect on the series of events leading up to the confrontation, or incident.

3. Ask yourself, what role did I play in this situation?

4. When you are ready to calmly address the person with whom you are in conflict, open by gently explaining how you felt when the person committed the offense.

5. Acknowledge any role that you played in the conflict.

Regardless of whether the person intended to offend you or not, they cannot dispute how it made you feel. Often times by starting a dialog with this approach, you both may realize it was a misunderstanding or miscommunication, and that in turn helps to diffuse the situation.

Not getting angry is not a realistic goal; it is as inevitable as the weather being hot in the southeast in the summer, and cold in the northeast in the winter. We don't approach either of these conditions by thinking the weather is not going to get hot or cold this year; instead we make adjustments to our responses. In the heat we do things such as consume more water, stay in the shade, and wear lighter clothing. In a similar way we must deal with our anger and manage conflicts by applying God's word and using the above steps.

Most importantly ask God for help in this area! It's not going to be easy but you can do it! With God all things are possible!

Bible Verse: Be kind and compassionate to one another, forgiving each other, just as in Christ God forgave you.—Ephesians 4:32, NIV

Heavenly Father, I come to You with great thanks for all that You do in my life. I ask that You fill me with patience and self-control to prevent me from acting out in anger toward others. Give me a gentle and kind spirit, and allow me to be a blessing to those who need encouragement. In Jesus' name I pray, Amen.

Chapter 14

Speak Life

WHEN I WAS IN the corporate world working in loss prevention, gossip was just about an everyday occurrence. Most of us are familiar with the expression "conversation at the water cooler" but in my experience it went to an entirely different level. The gossip was often mean-spirited and involved cutting people down. It was a competitive working environment where many people behaved as if the more they made others look bad, the better they thought they would look. This is basically the opposite of what the Bible teaches, but during this period of time I don't think I ever read the Bible at all. Yes I attended Catholic school for six years, but the Bible wasn't encouraged—not that I would have put any effort into it anyway.

Ironically my office was right across from the water cooler so what better location to hear the daily late afternoon gossip sessions. Friday afternoons in particular were a big day for gossip get-togethers. Later I realized that my office was not the only meeting hub; some of the participants traveled from office to office basically taking their gossiping "on the road." In our corporate office almost all of the offices had glass fronts so you could clearly see inside.

When I began my walk with the Lord, started really reading the word of God, and applying Biblical principles to my life, I felt a strong conviction about gossiping, also referred to as backbiting in the Bible. When I would hear people talking about someone in a negative manner, it grated on my nerves like nails on a chalkboard. I still caught myself falling into it from time to time, however I made every effort to pull myself away from such situations.

During the past three years I have been blessed to be working in a Christian program with other believers. Certainly we are not perfect, but when I am away from a Christian environment, I notice a huge difference between the culture of my organization and that of the world.

As an example, while writing this book I attended a conference and I was really excited about the speakers as well as seeing some people who were attending. While I was checking in, I ran into an old friend and within minutes she began trashing the venue and the speakers. One of them was someone I had been looking forward to hearing. Shortly thereafter I was with some other people and the same type of negative conversation started again. I noticed that I started having doubts in my own mind about how good the conference was going to be and it hadn't even started yet! I went from all pumped up about this event to a much more reserved outlook. My point is that we want to be around people with a positive outlook who speak life into us, not negativity. In this way we will be encouraged to seek out the best in every situation.

Apostle Paul writes in 1 Corinthians 15:33, "Do not be misled: Bad Company corrupts good character" (NIV). With this truth in mind you may want to take a look at the people who are around you. If they gossip and talk critically about others, you can rest assured they are doing the same about you when you are not around. I also notice that when I bring up a person who has wronged me in the past and begin to talk about them, it just makes me feel uneasy inside.

Sometimes it's not a question of unforgiveness, but simply unpleasant to have to think or talk about. Why bring up negative issues from the past anyway, what positive purpose does it serve to dredge these things up? Personally, I do not enjoy spending a lot of time around people who do this either. I would encourage you to try to avoid speaking about past wrongs and surrounding yourself with people who are positive, people who focus on their blessings instead of constantly criticizing everything and everyone around them. This does not have to mean moving into a cabin in the mountains by yourself, it's just a way of ensuring that bad company is not corrupting your character. As the saying goes, life is short. When I was younger, I never gave that much thought. Now as I am getting older, it has much more significance to me. I spent way too many years in the darkness of depression and negativity, and the last thing I want to do is be around it now.

That's not to say we are not to be there for those who are suffering, that is actually what I do for a living now and it is incredibly rewarding. I draw from my own difficult experiences on a daily basis in an attempt to encourage others. The past does not own me, God has freed me from it through His word, and I have realized that God wants me to use my own past struggles to help others in a positive way. He loves to turn a negative into a positive. This is explained in Romans 8:28, "And we know that all things work together for good to those who love God, to those who are called according to His purpose" (NKJV). God can heal our past sufferings and use our experiences for good in the future.

My word of caution to you about the potential of bad company to corrupt good character is about carefully considering whom you include in your inner circle of close friends. If we model Jesus, we see that He choose twelve disciples and they were all together for the three years of his ministry. However, of those twelve, there were only three who we can say were in His inner circle: Peter, John, and James. They are the ones with whom He would spend private time talking and praying. In fact, the disciple John who wrote the gospel of the same name, referred to himself not as John, but as the disciple whom Jesus loved.

Therefore, I encourage you to move past the gossip and began to speak to people wholly in truth and love. You will begin to notice that most people will respond in kind.

Bible Verse: Do not let any unwholesome talk come out of your mouths, but only what is helpful for building others up according to their needs, that it may benefit those who listen.—Ephesians 4:29, NIV

Heavenly Father, You are the one who strengthens me when I am weak. You are where I find comfort. Help me to keep my eyes fixed on You and Your ways. I want to be more like You, but I continue to fall short. Please fill me with Your presence so I can be a blessing to others and bring glory to Your kingdom. In Jesus' name I pray, Amen.

Chapter 15

Redirecting My Thoughts

For many years I often put much emphasis on negative situations or the negative aspect of situations, many of which were actually good. Maybe you can relate. The Apostle Paul wrote, "We demolish arguments and every pretension that sets itself up against the knowledge of God, and we take captive every thought to make it obedient to Christ" (2 Corinthians 10:5, NIV).

According to this biblical truth we are to take our thoughts captive! If you think about it, the word *captive* means someone or something that is kept in confinement. If you apply this to your life, you will begin the process of taking control of your own thoughts, rather than allowing them to control you. You will probably agree that you can only have one thought at a time, so with that being the case, you can begin to interrupt the negative thoughts by doing something other than feeding them. Try interrupting the negative thought process by praying, journaling, reading, listening to music, or talking to someone—anything other than giving them power by continuing to focus on them. We sometimes spend too much time on the problem—which is often us—rather than the solution, which is God. Proverbs 23:7 tells us, "For as he thinketh in his heart, so is he" (KJV).

King Solomon wrote that proverb and biblical scholars consider him the wisest man who ever lived. This verse leads me to conclude that if I am consumed in my heart with negative thoughts, I will, in turn, become negative. If I am consumed in my heart with stressful thoughts, I will be stressed. If I am consumed with sad thoughts, I will be saddened. And so the pattern continues: as you think, so you shall be. This applies to any thoughts that you allow to consume you, negative or positive.

Let's say you go to a conference with one hundred people in attendance and you only watch five people who are having a horrible time. You will leave there saying it was a horrible event. The reality might have been that ninety-five out of the one hundred people were having a great time but you were only focused on the negative aspects of this event. The same thing is true with your thought life. Don't get bogged down focusing on a few negative details. Instead, focus on all of the many blessings that God has given you.

You can start by interrupting the negative thoughts and redirecting your focus. In this way, you will begin to take control of your thoughts and your life. It will not be easy at first, but as you continue to put this into practice I can confidently say that you will see positive results. If I can do it, anyone can.

Bible Verse: Don't copy the behavior and customs of this world, but let God transform you into a new person by changing the way you think. Then you will learn to know God's will for you, which is good and pleasing and perfect.—Romans 12:2, NLT

Heavenly Father, I ask for complete transformation and empowerment to change the way I think about every situation. Help me to keep my mind fixed on You, and Your amazing love and mercy. In Jesus name I pray, Amen.

Chapter 16

What Was My Role in the Conflict?

AT THE RISK OF sounding shallow, let me confess that for about three months I drove forty-five minutes to get my hair cut. Why would I do that? Well, I prefer barbers to salons and after many attempts I had finally found a really good one. When I had initially started going to this particular barbershop I only lived five minutes away, but I had since moved, and had not yet found a new barber in my local neighborhood.

On one particular Saturday I had made an appointment for a much-needed haircut with my main barber. About an hour after scheduling the appointment I called back and rescheduled for a later time. When I arrived my barber was not there. Another employee told me that he would be right back, and that I should stay there and wait a few minutes. Even though they told me to stay, I decided to go to the awesome deli next door. During my absence, my barber had returned, and had been waiting for me. Unable to wait any longer, he eventually he stepped out to make a phone call. When I arrived back at the shop and saw that my barber was still not there, I became really angry. I realized that I was probably going to miss my next engagement due to the delay. Sitting in the shop waiting for him to return again provided me with the opportunity to think about the events leading up to my frustration. As I sat I also had time to reflect on my own role in the situation. First, I had rescheduled the appointment after my initial call. Second, I had left to go to the deli after being advised to stay and wait, and this had caused me to miss him again.

As I sat there and considered my own actions, I realized that I had become irritated and was likely about to take it out on him when in reality the entire situation was my fault. This realization allowed me to develop a strategy for delaying my reactions and fully considering each situation in a biblical context before acting out of pure emotion. Since that time, I began to encourage the clients at the Christian treatment center where I work to practice three of the five simple steps I provided earlier when they feel upset with someone:

1. Take some time to calm down before speaking to the person you feel has upset you.

2. Reflect on the series of events leading up to the confrontation, or incident.

3. Ask yourself, what role did I play in this situation?

Be open to consider that you might be partially or fully responsible for the issue, as I found myself to be. You will often find some area where you contributed to a conflict, and when you employ self-control by carefully considering the circumstances—putting yourself in the other person's position—it allows you to achieve greater wisdom about what occurred and it becomes much easier to resolve differences.

Bible Verse: Whoever conceals their sins does not prosper, but the one who confesses and renounces them finds mercy.—Proverbs 28:13, NIV

Heavenly Father, I ask for a pure heart and a restored mind, a mind that is fixed on You, and the truth of Your word. Give me patience and understanding to calmly reflect on each challenging situation that I encounter. Help me to respond to every conflict in a way that is pleasing to You. In Jesus' name I pray, Amen.

Chapter 17

Name Above All Names

THE MORE I READ the Bible, the more I begin to understand the awesome power of the name of Jesus. I also think about the fact that so many people are offended by His name, including some Christians who shy away from using it in conversation around non-believers. They will say God, but not Jesus because perhaps they feel that may offend someone.

It is really strange how His name can have such an effect on people. All of the angels worship Him and all the demons tremble at His name, yet here on earth people often times curse His name or shy away from using it for fear of coming across as politically incorrect.

Due to this fact, this next verse may not be as popular as others, but here is what Jesus said in Matthew 10:33, "But everyone who denies me here on earth, I will also deny before my Father in heaven" (NLT).

Why would people become so outraged by the mention of the name Jesus? Even if you do not believe that He is the Son of God or that He rose from the dead on the third day, and you only believe He was a good teacher or prophet like many other religious figures, why the outrage? I believe the reason is a spiritual one.

I am blessed to be a good friend of John Ramirez who was at one time a high-level devil worshipper for twenty-five years. He is now a devout, international, Christian evangelist, and author of the popular books *Out of the Devil's Cauldron, Unmasking the Devil,* and most recently, *Armed and Dangerous.* For the past sixteen years, John has been training pastors and faith leaders on the dangers of the kingdom of darkness and how to fight this very real spiritual battle.

I have attended a number of John's services and I have witnessed pure evil up close. The first time I was invited by him to attend one of his services where he ministers to people afflicted by demonic influence, I was surprised to see that these people appeared normal prior to going up to the altar. In fact, I was talking to some of them before the deliverance took place.

Please understand that evil exists and the devil is relentless in trying to destroy people. This is especially true if we give him an opening through occult activity such as Ouija boards, tarot cards, palm reading, or attempting to connect with the dead through mediums. Even habitual sin such as unforgiveness can make us vulnerable to the enemy. Such practices are open invitations for him to initiate a spiritual attack against you, and he will turn your life upside down.

The Apostle Paul writes in Ephesians 6:10–18,

> "Finally, my brethren, be strong in the Lord and in the power of His might. Put on the whole armor of God, that you may be able to stand against the wiles of the devil. For we do not wrestle against flesh and blood, but against principalities, against powers, against the rulers

of the darkness of this age, against spiritual hosts of wickedness in the heavenly places. Therefore take up the whole armor of God that you may be able to withstand in the evil day, and having done all, to stand. Stand therefore, having girded your waist with truth, having put on the breast-plate of righteousness, and having shod your feet with the preparation of the gospel of peace; above all, taking the shield of faith with which you will be able to quench all the fiery darts of the wicked one. And take the helmet of salva-tion, and the sword of the Spirit, which is the word of God; praying always with all prayer and supplication in the Spirit, being watchful to this end with all perseverance and supplication for all the saints" (NKJV).

I believe it is a spiritual influence that leads people to become outraged by the name of Jesus, and this is illus-trated by the fact that, "we do not wrestle against flesh and blood." Paul is saying that the fight is not about people; the fight is a spiritual battle. How do we combat something that we cannot see? We must put on the full armor of God and use the word of God (the Bible) as our offensive weapon.

Now this all may seem strange to start focusing on the kingdom of darkness, and even many churches are reluc-tant to teach on it because for many it's simply too strange or scary. It is not a popular topic and it certainly won't fill up the pews, but the reality is that Jesus spoke more about demons and hell than he did about angels and heaven. Jesus himself was the first one to cast out demons, so why then did he put such an emphasis on evil? I would submit that he did so because He wants us to be aware that we have a very real enemy who is out to destroy us, and he wants us to know the devil's methods so we can avoid becoming victims. Just because you choose to believe that Satan and demons are not real does not keep you safe from them, and it definitely does not exclude you from the battle.

The devil has immense hatred toward God but he is powerless against Him. Therefore he attacks us because we are made in the image of God. Consider Genesis 1:27, "So God created mankind in his own image, in the image of God he created them; male and female he created them" (NIV). With this in mind, wouldn't you want to know your enemy's tactics? I know I would. This does not mean we give darkness more power; we have complete authority over all of it through Christ. It simply means we are aware of its existence and put on the armor of God for the battle.

Jesus explains that the enemy of God's people (the devil) seeks to do us harm, but that He is here to give us strength in John 10:10, "The thief does not come except to steal, and to kill, and to destroy. I have come that they may have life, and that they may have it more abundantly" (NKJV). As believers, we cannot disregard verses that might make us feel uncomfortable. Furthermore, we would be wise to heed Jesus' warnings on this controversial topic. If you are someone who is inclined to dismiss Jesus' teachings on this subject, I would encourage you to pray about it and ask God to increase your faith and understanding of these biblical truths.

If you are embarrassed or timid when it comes to speaking about Jesus, ask Him for a sense of boldness so you can be a voice for Christ to those who are suffering and broken in spirit. He is looking for people to use and to help him share His message of hope.

Bible Verse: Therefore God also has highly exalted Him and given Him the name which is above every name, that at the name of Jesus every knee should bow, of those in heaven, and of those on earth, and of those under the earth, and that every tongue should confess that Jesus Christ is Lord, to the glory of God the Father.—Philippians 2:9–11, NKJV

Heavenly Father, I give You thanks and praise for Your Son Jesus and I acknowledge that His name is above all names. Give me a boldness to proclaim this beautiful truth to the world without fear of any consequences or negative responses. Keep me safe from the evil one as I proclaim the name above all names, Jesus Christ. In Jesus' name I pray, Amen.

Chapter 18

Building Spiritual Muscle

MANY TIMES WE PUT tremendous focus on our physical appearance yet very little effort into our spiritual life. For example, consider any situation or individual that upsets you. You may be unable to control the situation, or how someone treats you, but you can control how you respond. Apostle Paul writes, "So I say, let the Holy Spirit guide your lives. Then you won't be doing what your sinful nature craves. The sinful nature wants to do evil, which is just the opposite of what the Spirit wants. And the Spirit gives us desires that are the opposite of what the sinful nature craves. These two forces are constantly fighting each other" (Galatians 5:16–17, NLT).

Paul also tells us in Galatians 5:22–23 that two of the fruits of the Spirit are patience and self-control (NLT). With these truths in mind, seek to rethink the offensive situation or individual who upsets, manipulates, hurts, or lies to you. To practice responding to such situations with patience and self-control builds spiritual muscle. At first, it may feel strange or difficult, but as you continue to employ God's word to your life, it will become easier. When you respond to difficult situations with patience and self-control, this emanates from the Holy Spirit. However, when you respond with negative emotions such as anger, hatred, or jealousy, these reactions are based in the sinful nature.

Look at it this way, the more you feed the spirit the stronger you become spiritually, hence the sinful nature becomes weaker. If you buy a plant and water it daily, it grows and becomes stronger. However, if you were to deprive that same plant of water, it would dry up, become weak, and eventually die. That is similar to what we want to do with our sinful nature. Do not feed those negative thoughts and responses, instead feed the positive spiritual responses that stem from patience and self-control.

You may remember the horrible story of former football star quarterback Michael Vick, who played in the National Football League. Vick ran an illegal dog-fighting ring. The dogs were all pit bulls that were trained to fight each other, often viciously to their deaths. People bet large amounts of money on the fights, often in the six-figure range. Obviously, with such large amounts of money at stake from illegal activities, you can *bet* that fights will be rigged to ensure wins for the organizers. During the raid of his compound, a reporter interviewed one of the dog handlers and asked him how they could be sure which dog would win each match. The handler explained that they knew because the dogs that they fed were the ones that would win. This struck me as horrific at the time, and I find it even more disturbing now having become the owner of a beautiful, loving, playful, pit bull terrier named Luke. It is truly a disgrace that some people would invest time and resources to turn something so good into something so vicious for evil purposes, all because they so readily gave in to their sinful nature.

The handler's disturbing response is a reminder for me of the powerful influence of feeding either the Spirit or the sinful nature. When we act or respond based on our sinful nature, we are satisfying our worldly desires that are in opposition to God's will. This typically involves making emotionally driven choices rather than spiritual ones. When we feed the Spirit, we are more aligned with God's will for our lives. This leads me to the question, which one are you feeding? I would encourage you to ask God to lead you by His spirit throughout your life.

Bible Verse: But the Holy Spirit produces this kind of fruit in our lives: love, joy, peace, patience, kindness, goodness, faithfulness, gentleness, and self-control. There is no law against these things!—Galatians 5:22–23, NLT

Heavenly Father, I ask for an increase in patience and self-control. Please help me to not react in anger, but always in a calm, controlled, and respectful manner. I ask you now to empower me to walk in the fruit of Your Spirit. In Jesus' name I pray, Amen.

Chapter 19

Closing Comments

I WOULD LIKE TO thank you for taking the time to read this book. It has truly been a blessing to write it and has also provided me the opportunity to reflect back on the countless expressions of God's incredible compassion, love, and mercy throughout my spiritual journey. I encourage you to apply God's word to every area of your life and to surrender your will to His will which is perfect.

May God bless and protect you and your family.

Sincerely,

Anthony Acampora